Carsten René Nielsen

Translated by David Keplinger

Selected Prose Poems

The World Cut Out
with Crooked Scissors

New Issues Poetry & Prose

A Green Rose Book

New Issues Poetry & Prose
The College of Arts and Sciences
Western Michigan University
Kalamazoo, Michigan 49008

First Edition, 2007.

ISBN-10   1-930974-70-1 (paperbound)
ISBN-13   978-1-930974-70-8 (paperbound)

Library of Congress Cataloging-in-Publication Data:
Nielsen, Carsten René
The World Cut Out with Crooked Scissors/Carsten René Nielsen
Library of Congress Control Number: 2007924972

Managing Editor   Marianne Swierenga
Copy Editor   Elizabeth Marzoni
Designer   Krystle Lilliesterna
Art Director   Tricia Hennessy
Production Manager   Paul Sizer
                         The Design Center, School of Art
                         College of Fine Arts
                         Western Michigan University

The World Cut Out with Crooked Scissors

Selected Prose Poems
Carsten René Nielsen

Translated by David Keplinger

New Issues

WESTERN MICHIGAN UNIVERSITY

Also by Carsten René Nielsen

Contents

From *Circles* (1998)

Underligt

> *The idiom is the lair of the tribal beast.*
> —Charles Simic

The challenge of translators is to build the ideal environment, an idiom for the poet's true voice to inhabit. That American poets like Robert Bly, W.S. Merwin, Rika Lesser, Coleman Barks, and Robert Hass have enjoyed such success as translators speaks of their abilities to nurture voices. Thus the poems of Vallejo, Neruda, Rilke, Rumi, and Milosz have good, permanent homes in the American idiom. They live among us. They have poet-children, many who have never read them in their native tongues. But that is not true for most translations. Translated voices rarely survive in captivity.

I hadn't considered this problem when, in the winter of 1995 in Copenhagen, I first heard the poems of Carsten René Nielsen improvisationally translated by a friend at his tiny apartment by the harbor. My friend read the lines aloud in Danish and then again in a choppy, hurried English. Even so, I was stunned by the clarity and originality of Nielsen's Blakean visions. I sensed their kinship to Rimbaud, Baudelaire, and Benjamin Perét. I sensed their debt to Charles Simic and Russell Edson (neither of whom, I learned, had Nielsen read before). But each next poem defied whatever categories I'd established for the last. In Danish the word is *underligt*, which means at once "peculiar" and, by its archaic root, "wonder-like." This voice, no matter the tradition it belonged to, indeed was wonder-like.

Returning to the United States I discovered that no English versions of Nielsen were available. I decided to contact the poet myself and inquire. Nielsen replied immediately. There was not, he said, a collection in English, but he would be willing to work with me to produce one. As I did not know Danish to fluency, Nielsen would translate rough, word-for-word versions of the poems. By e-mail, he would accompany them with notes and notes and notes. My versions of his versions were sent back with additional notes. This continued for nine years, until now, when his latest three books are presented for American readers to enjoy for the first time anywhere.

Born in 1966, Nielsen works as a full time writer in Aarhus, the second largest Danish city, an academic and cultural center located on the peninsula of Jutland. Aarhus is also the home of the Grauballe Man, a bog man 2000 years old and displayed year round at Moesgaard Museum in a wooded area south of the city. This man, his cut open throat, his fractured shin, his beard stubble, his skin—even his fingerprints—preserved by the tannins of the bog, though flattened by its tremendous weight, lies displayed under glass, a ghastly testament to our common tribal past. I find in Nielsen's poems a similar spectacle—the little glass box of form, and, within, something old, nasty, fascinating, human. "Up from blackened mould the hair is growing," says the hideous, archetypal barber in "Hair." Like the Grauballe Man, the people and animals and places of these poems remain both here and not here, both present and ancient in their manifest forms.

And I sense a little sleight of hand at work, too. A magician, dressed in that old fashioned getup, the poet flips the real into illusions; illusions into the real. What's inside that closet? I ask myself. Is it the horrible? The beautiful? The closet must and does contain both possibilities. Here we meet the ordered, decorous nineteenth century, as backdrop to the frantic spontaneity of the twenty-first. The poems have neither beginnings nor endings. Nielsen is insatiable, the meta-poet of "The Poet" who aches "to put it another way." He distracts us with references to science and history, art, or with personal memories. It's a wonderful show. Here is a magician who can disassemble worlds: using just that magic wand, that cape, that good saw.

David Keplinger
January, 2007

From *Forty-One Animals* (2005)

Spider

A puppet theater composed entirely of spiders. It's Macbeth, performed by the fat boy of the class. He has dressed all in black and can hardly be seen behind his theater box in the darkened classroom. The rods from which the spiders are hung, and the many threads that steer their movements, he controls with fabulous precision, a cool passion, and he does all the lines himself in different voices. The witches are played by three fat garden spiders. "Fair is foul, and foul is fair," they cackle, but none of the children pay attention. The boys are shouting, and the girls are screaming hysterically. Nor does the teacher see the beauty in the performance. In all the turmoil her only concern is finding the switch for the lights.

Dormouse

One must be arrogant and dismissive whenever meeting a dormouse. Otherwise, it nestles down to sleep inside the groove between one's chin and lower lip. There it stays until one grows a beard, and by then it's absolutely impossible to get rid of. The whiskers on a dormouse are long and thick, and when you kiss a pretty girl, she will find it quite unpleasant. If she doesn't say anything, it's because she is truly in love. But only the dormouse knows with whom.

Octopus

On the bottom of the basin by the old oil harbor lies a giant octopus. In its eight arms it holds a sea mine, which it gently rocks back and forth as it sings. It's an older contact mine, a horned mine with an explosive charge of one hundred and twenty kilos of TNT. The dock workers claim there's no reason to be afraid: octopi can live for more than two hundred years, and their lullabys consist of at least four thousand verses. They're full of it, of course. Just ask the one-legged clerk at the fishmonger's shop. He will tell how his false teeth, even long after he's taken them out in the evening, keep chattering in their waterglass.

Black-Headed Gull

When the seagulls have laid their eggs in the socks that are hung out to dry in the back yard, they fly to the park, where they make a helix, a perfect formation, over the statue of the naked, young girl. Exactly as the gull droppings fall on the copper crown of her head, the model for the statue stands in her room in the nursing home, fencing with her own reflection in the mirror.

Lizard

Lizards can shine faintly in the dark, and because the terns feed their young with live lizards, in the evening you may be so lucky, through the light-sensitive optics of night glasses, to catch them shining in flight. Their wings move like oar-strokes of light in the darkness. Not that such a thing could impress my father, who once caught a lizard with seven tails. He kept the proof of his feat stored in spirits, inside jam jars: in one glass lay the tails and in another the body of the lizard. I only remember the glass with the tails, though. Like most modern families my parents lived apart, and it was my mother who took the rest of the animal. Now, as both my parents are dead, I have the two glasses standing on a shelf above my writing desk. Guess it's just human nature: you imagine the animal is lying in one glass, missing its tails in the other.

Hare

Sitting in the field is a hare. It can hear a mouse peeing far away; it clearly sees the crow's lone flight feather slowly fall through clouds at dusk. If you listen to the trees with a stethoscope, you hear them sigh. For each step you get nearer the horizon, you will weigh a little less, but there is no reason to start moving. If you remain motionless, you are, from the perspective of the hare, already as good as weightless.

Elephant

The elephant on the mural in the Church of Birkerød is highly unusual. It has no trunk, but rather a snout in the shape of a horn on an old gramophone. It's slender as a racehorse; its thick tail splits into three. Instead of hoove-like nails, it has on its feet four elaborately curving claws of ivory. In contrast, it has no tusks, and its neck is equipped with large, serrated scales like a crocodile's. Most of all I love its round white eyes, each with a great black pupil, lending it a sad and at the same time utterly baffled expression. Like it knows that it's been painted all wrong.

Frog

Here's how it would be: spring, the windows would be open, the frogs jumping around the living room. "Not so close to the chandelier, little friends, and don't you shit in Auntie Marianne's hair!" Outside, the beech tree is ready to take off. We watch the neighbor strike the match and light the fuse, which fizzles all the way to the trunk. But nothing happens. The tree stays where it is. In silence we behold it from the window under an almost transparent sun. In the sky, above the city downtown, floats a green frog as big as a zeppelin.

Butterfly

What a blunder it was to strike the word *wigwam* on the poster for the traveling carnival, and instead, in the cursive of a schoolgirl, to write the word *vagina*. And who could have known that so many people would like to spend the night there? It had to be something psychological, thought the ringleader of the carnival. He himself would get quadruple vision if somebody mentioned the word *turnip*. The queue stretched from the fairground all the way down to the harbor, where at the back could be seen a captain of the merchant navy with a butterfly, a beautiful swallowtail with spread-out wings, fastened with a pin to his lapel.

Water Vole

In 1711 the inhabitants of the village Als by the Fjord of Mariager took out a writ against the water voles, and, to play it safe, all rats, moles, gophers, and mice were summoned as well, with eight days notice to appear before the magistrate: "For grievances, wherein witnesses shall answer inquiries referring to all said illegal and irreparable damage which the accused on our grain, fields, meadows and grasslands, have begotten and upturned." The water voles were appointed a lawyer, but the night before the announced trial they tunneled through the churchyard end to end. By morning the graves had caved in, the hedges and gravestones had collapsed, and across the churchyard could be seen body parts and bones protruding from the ground. It's said that the skulls, which were never identified, still lie in a box in the attic of the rectory. Tied to each head is a tag where a large question mark is written in ink.

Fox

Already an unusual day at the feather cleaning unit. First a glassy, nearly weightless bird that resembled a stork, then a goose with an underside shaped like a flowerpot. And now someone's turned in a fox with the plumage of a kestrel. Days like these he dreams of quitting. How he'd stand in the office and utter the words, then walk to the parking lot in the pale morning and finally be free. But he also knows he won't do it. Financially, it isn't possible. He has a photo of his wife and their three children in his wallet, and, on a day like this, he takes it out and gazes at their smiling faces. It provides a certain comfort, although someone has drawn moustaches on all three of them.

Hen

In the kitchen, in a colander in the sink: a boiled hen with no feathers. It blinks, it is still alive. White ashes shower from sparkling clouds. "What a nightmare," says the woman, relieved, as she folds up her umbrella. She stands on the beach and now looks at the sun, which slowly sinks into the ocean. At the same time, on the golf course, a man carefully adjusts an egg on the tee.

Squirrel

The zoologists, they write that the squirrel is the most elegant rodent. With tactile hair on its wrist and along the arm, there even exists a squirrel so ticklish that when it climbs trees it produces the characteristic high-pitched click with the tongue, which is a squirrel's version of laughter. Conversely, one squirrel is continually overlooked when the rest are accounted for. That particular squirrel's to blame when, on rare occasions, one sees an apple tree with only cores dangling from the branches.

Hedgehog

When one of the lunatics succeeded in training his imaginary hedgehog, panic broke out in the asylum. That month each and every patient bled from small wounds on their hands and feet. It was a matter of collective stigmatization, explained the staff, who behaved as if nothing was happening. The doctors just sat with feet raised at their meetings, and, every so often, you'd see a nurse quickly do a few dance steps, a couple of small elegant dance steps, as she conducted her rounds through the ward. "Years later, I was still finding holes in my handkerchiefs," the retired chief physician told me. Since then, he'd written all his letters with invisible ink.

Parrot

In a pet shop twelve parrots march in a circle. One parrot with speed-lines beside the eyes, another with a yellow mustache, a third carries the sun on its back. On a chair in the center of the circle sits a woman dressed as the Virgin Mary in Raphael's *Madonna del Granduca*. A naked boy child lies over her knee, and she has her right hand raised. Each time a parrot says that it wants sugar, she hits the child hard on the bottom. Right outside on the street in front of the shop an old, hunchbacked woman is sweeping the sidewalk. It is she one must approach discretely, if one is bringing sugar for the parrots.

Okapi

Equipped with half-masks and corks in their ears, many completely tone-deaf people indulge in levitating during the performances of operas. It's the latest thing, it requires only a nose pincher. Afterwards, one might on rare occasions suffer a toothache, but most can still say, though with a somewhat nasal voice, "ahoy okapi," and without any trouble open an umbrella and float down from the balcony. Until 1901 only the indigenous peoples deep inside the jungle of Congo knew about the okapi, related to the giraffe. Word is, it has fabulous hearing. I myself have a head filled with helium, but heights are not my thing. I'd much prefer a good run in the woods chasing the okapi, usually made to graze in the orchestra pit.

Milking Cow

"Without it there will be no milk, without it there will be no milk," echoes the farmer's words in the head of the cow. The farmer has unscrewed a spark plug from one of its teats, and he presents it smiling to the amazed children on a field trip. The spark plug belongs to a milk truck, one of those enormous milk trucks, larger than tankers, that careens down Jutland on the motorways, the small cars maneuvering between its gigantic wheels. As the milk truck leaves the farmyard and disappears in a cloud of dust, the cow envisions itself as old: it is so thin, the farmer has been forced to fasten its skin to its body with pins. The last thing it hears is a girl who asks what will happen should someone unfasten the pins.

Trade Rat

Once I had everything, was naive and happy as could be, but my most beautiful possession, my dried starfish, was exchanged for an old button. Instead of my stuffed toad, whom I loved to gaze at since it didn't gaze at anything, I found a ticket to a horse-drawn trolley. My cap disappeared, and on my head was placed a raspberry. I tried to set a snare for this invisible rat, *Neotoma floridana*, but before long I stepped into a bear trap. I attempted to relieve my sorrow and my anger with medicine, but was given an etiquette book instead. Now I'm utterly ruined, and a withered leaf lies in my chest in the place where my heart used to be.

House Mouse

He who thinks he's got it all figured out will often end up playing too much with mice. You see it clearly in ones who are missing parts of their bodies. It happens slowly, because the mice take only small bites, but you can still easily lose both arms from the wrist up to the shoulder, so that only the hands remain. And look, now it's you the sage is waving to! Blow a soap bubble with a mousetrap inside, give him a bump on the head, a haystack served as breakfast in bed. Tell him there are screws in September, syringes in October. He will not understand it. It's the mice: they're nesting in his cranium.

Herring

Today there is an astonishing light. One can see far down into the ocean, where the few remaining herring are all wearing wigs. Once it would be teeming here with girls removing the gills and women salting the fish down. But on the beach now: just one woman, sunning herself. She is naked; has her navel between her legs; her teeth are made of wood. She shouts: "Good herring here!" and sticks out her tongue as she sees me approach in my pajamas. I simply answer that at least I'm still breathing, thank you very much! Later I sense something wrong with the tongue: the tongue was a herring.

Griffon Vulture

Under a sun inside a sun the vultures begin to circle. As always they show themselves only in profile. As always they look only to the left. In the cellar in a house beneath them lies a mummified cat lit up by camera flashes. The whole scene smacks of eroticism and decadence. The glass of water on the night table beside the divan up in the bedroom, where a young naked girl lies stretched out with a poisonous snake in her hand, has been standing there for millennia. It's strange: if it isn't the sound of the surf against faraway shores you hear when you open her drawers, why spit over your left shoulder when a black cat passes the road? I mean: who other than vultures are interested in how long you can hold your breath in a house where you drink no water?

Carrier Pigeon

Don't worry about me. This is not a poem about poetry. It is just so boring to wait for those carrier pigeons. But somebody has to do it. How else could they manage to weather the storm with the letters the two lovers keep returning to each other "address unknown?" Somebody has to do it, and that somebody is me. I have to sit here by my desk with rolled-up shirt sleeves and greased-down hair. When the mail has been postmarked and the pigeons have had their water and feed, I sometimes sit and wonder what's in those letters? "You have transformed my heart into an hourglass without sand." Or: "For each moment we are not together, my shadow becomes more and more transparent." So don't worry. When the same two letters cross my desk again, something utterly different will be written in them.

Dog

After hours the midwife feeds her dogs umbilical cords from the newborns. For Christmas they get a little sucking pig, still alive. She is of the old school, always keeps the Bible and a jam jar with leeches in her black handbag. "Isn't it cruelty to animals?" ask my two nieces in wonder, as they crawl about looking for their gifts under the tree. To this I can't answer in any other way than with a classic tragic gesture: I throw my head back, lift one arm up to my face and lay the back of my hand against my forehead. To that not a word, just a prolonged sigh, which is almost drowned out by the baying of dogs from the yard.

Sheep

"*Putain,*" one of the Siamese twins angrily whispers to the other, mute from birth and, like me, a first time guest in the museum that exhibits animals only as we see them in dreams. Her knee touches mine as we sit on a bench and watch sheep after sheep jump over a hedge. The sheep are sheared into shapes like paints thrown from a short distance against a canvas. While I wait for the talking twin to fall asleep, I imagine what the sheep resemble: an explosion of honey in a beehive, milkweed grown without the influence of gravity, an orchid with lungs. But in the end it's me whom the old guard wakes: "We're closing now," he says, and clips my tie with a hole-puncher before sleep-drunk I'm led to the exit.

Lion

At the circus we see an unusually skillful lion tamer. Classically dressed in striped strong-man tights, completely bald and with a handlebar moustache. He holds a watering can in his hand. Cautiously, oh so cautiously, he pours water in the ears of a lion. A deaf lion is quite harmless. With no danger he can call it names: "Kayak upholstery, rocking-chair-ballast, potato testicle!" Most dangerous is if the lion has to sneeze. The trick is to pinch it by the nose until the water fills up its eyes.

Pig

A pig with a gas mask and an armband with a swastika around its left foreleg. Something is written in Hebrew on one side of the pig. A man dressed as an Arab shovels hand grenades into its trough with a pitch-fork. It is all very political, very *avant garde*. Throughout the audience the pickpockets are engaged in the evening's racket: to lift the wallets from pockets, wrap them into cellophane and, without incident, replace them. After the performance the pig is cut up, and some very fine pork chops are sold at a reasonable price. If you ask the butcher, he'll just shrug his shoulders: he's seen it all before.

Owl

I am in the gymnasium lifting dumbbells up to the chest. It's the best thing I know: when even the brain is a sparkling muscle, a pumping lung. An owl has landed on my shoulder and bites my earlobe while whispering obscenities. If this were the dark continent on the other side of the Atlantic and not enlightened Europe, I would be burnt as a witch at the stake. Now it begins its good-humored allegories, stories about abominable downpours of acid rain and upright skeletons of giraffes. What does it see that I don't see? I just lift the dumbbells up to the chest. It's the best thing I know: when the roof and walls of the building become transparent, and when the plains, the rivers and the woods emerge around me. Already in a corner of the gymnasium a football has turned into glass.

Horse

While she does her rounds in the stable, the girl just for a moment senses one of the horses is puckering, as if it whistles a few bars by sucking air in, instead of blowing out. At closer look, the horse just gazes onward with a dull expression, chewing cud.

Wild Boar

On the bottom of the ocean, in the singing school for mummies, the teacher ties the tongues of his students into knots. While they chirp through their noses, wild boars root through the seabed outside. I would so much like to lie there with you in the rutting season of the boar under the mighty crowns of the beech trees, in which the dolphins are playing. Each morning we'd pluck a truffle from each other's mouths, and everything would be declared a draw. Only the bubbles ever-rising from the noses of the mummies would disturb this idyll.

Zebra

The truth is nothing more than a collateral circumstance to beauty, and it is true that nothing is better than those moments when you suddenly are swimming in the senselessness of it all, stop in the middle of the street, see this flicker, the mosaics of the house fronts, the coarse weave of shadows, the rhythm of the breaches and cracks. Even the air is made of transparent blocks, crystalline gratings, which criss-cross each other and everything you see. Even the herd of zebras that stops mid-street, waiting patiently for the light to change, makes no sense.

Rat

Not a starfish caught in a spider's web, a raven in a bucket with wallpaper glue, an antelope influenced by laughing gas, nor a snail in a hunting bugle. Nothing can attract rats like a lump of cheese screwed into a lamp socket. I know this from back home, where it was also said that the rats wear mourning veils when there is nothing left in the larder. Back home a family like mine could be so poor, it had to live on fried rats. To this very day I still prefer to watch television, although tonight there are rats on all the channels again: rats who play the trumpet and bagpipes, a rat with pointed shoes and small bells on its cap, rats dressed in uniforms and suits. It's like nobody remembers how it was anymore. When only rat tail was left on the plate.

Sea Lion

They've tried to fake everything: the bark on the trees, the fur of the animals, the perfect beauty. Then, the projector is started, and we are watching a nature film about the mighty shoals of fish that with sudden shifts in direction thrust through the water. As if the fish had one common consciousness. After the film there is, at first, complete silence. Then the sea lions, who sit in the back row, begin to utter these characteristic, abrupt howls in their barking voices, clapping enthusiastically with their flipper-like forelimbs.

Minnow

The German zoologist von Frisch used minnows for experiments concerning the hearing of fish, proving that their hearing "is fully on the level of a not too musical human being." Minnows live in the upper brooks, where the water streams fast and clear, where the bottom is gravelled and stony, and where the music they are capable of experiencing with their primitive, synaesthetic senses, is the fleeting shapes and blurred images created by the refraction of the sunlight in the streaming water. It can resemble late fruit trees seen through a lens out of focus, or nebulous figures in long, loose robes floating through the water with outstretched hands.

Lapwing

In a chest of drawers with seven hundred drawers, each a different shape and size, lies a lapwing's egg somewhere. The thief is a freckled twelve-year-old girl who has to find the egg before the sun goes down. She knows that if she finds the egg and breaks it into her face, the freckles will disappear. But in the drawers she opens there is only water, only cheeping lapwing chicks. She climbs higher and higher, drawer over drawer, and finally just one drawer's left, at the very top, and the sun has now almost vanished. But it sticks, and she pulls and toils and tugs with her spindly arms, thrusts her feet against it, heaves and yanks and begins to cry. Then at last the drawer gives. It's been inserted upside down, and an egg falls out and onto the floor. With despair she stares at the egg as the lapwings start shrieking. They are all hand puppets made of old socks, and we, who hide behind the furniture in the living room, have to hold up a hand to our mouths not to laugh.

Marmot

Twenty thousand marmots sleep in the deserted city. They can be found everywhere in the deserted streets, on the sidewalks, on the benches and on the café tables among half-filled coffee cups and plates with bits of food left over. They sleep in each and every baby carriage, strewn at random throughout the promenade, they sleep in the giant urns for flowers, and in the garden beds. In the abandoned cars, with doors opened-wide in the middle of the streets, and in the shops on the shelves, in the showcases and in the deli cases the marmots lie sleeping. Only every fourth minute do they breathe. Only three times each minute do their hearts beat. At rare intervals it happens that a marmot wakes up, it stretches out, voids its bladder, and then goes back to sleep. Otherwise, all is hushed in the city.

Albatross

Just as the taxidermist lifts the majestic wings of the albatross to remove more of the giblets, the room grows dark. Without my seeing it, a sleeping potion is poured into my glass. I dream that we sleep in fields of feathers. Scissors thunder across the sky, but we know it's our task to draw the feathers from the ground by their shafts. Not until we are finished are we permitted to kiss. But, as they say, love overcomes all things. So on a naked globe we stand, all alone in the world, two children with closed eyes, lips pursed for a kiss.

From *Clairobscur* (2001)

Questionnaire

You are lying in the dizzyingly high grass. You remember it as an aurora borealis, an insignificant, brief happiness. Or: you are thirsty and dream about melting glaciers, chipped cisterns, reservoirs without boundary, nights on your back on irrigated fields. Or: you have fallen in love with the world and sit in a library with the first edition of the Belgian astronomer Quételet's catalogue of 10,792 stars, a register of all the world's totem animals, a book on mushrooms that grow only under our duvets at night, a natural history of the glove. Or: You are here. Right now.

Early

This poem is dedicated to the one who stands as a slender shadow on thin, staggering legs, behind the grate far into the yard, when you pass the gateway so early in the morning that the birds still have only one eye each.

Teeth

The dentist counts the teeth in three/four time. The assistant keeps track on the abacus. Those teeth that have the purest sound are best. I am the doll who lies in the chair with arms limp and the head tilted on its side. It could be the drainpipes that sing in the sun, the summer rain that moves away from earth: transparent, luminous nails that disappear into the wall of the universe. But it's the other way around: actually it's I who reclines in the light, and I am afraid that my teeth are so brittle they will sift away as a delicate, white pharmaceutical powder when the drilling starts. "We are doing this one in silver," says the dentist, but that doesn't seem quite natural. I too was built from skeleton parts found in the peat bog, the most garbled, oceanic, animal shapes. That's how it should always be. It's that simple.

Birds

In the botanical gardens the ornithologists sit in barrelsfull of earthworms. When you pass, you can see their watchful, wandering eyes that peek out right above the edge of the barrel. Each time a cloud hides the sun, tiny, tiny birds fly out of the mouths of the sun-bathing girls, who yawn as they wake looking up to estimate the size of the cloud. The birds seem to know that they are being watched and do their best to fly carelessly, elegantly. As if the world were just a stage set for their sake alone.

Shadow

The contours are absorbed in different intensities of light and in the indistinct regions between light and darkness everything is clear: wax candles flicker in a changing wind. The women store their dresses away. Somebody is sneaking down the stairs in stockinged feet. In the foreground you see a boy who stares at a sun draped with heavy velvet hangings in the thousand known nuances of gray. The clouds hang far away as frail bells.

Illumination

It is evening, and children costumed as children ring all the doorbells in the neighborhood, but nobody answers: their parents lie in open coffins that are slowly driven through the street on gun carriages drawn by blind horses. The streetlights are extinguished in respect for the dead, whose translucent bodies are full of radioactive tracers and light up in the dark.

Nature Morte

Because the leaves wither and soon no longer produce any oxygen, we shout down into an increasingly deeper crevasse. Only a solitary cyclist is seen hanging a few meters below, still with his bicycle, a vintage model, under him. We knock on the floors, but nobody answers. Me, I remember now that my father lies buried beneath the Astro-turf in the sports hall, that my mother lies drowned on the bottom of the Olympic-sized pool. When I meet them in my dreams, and they remove the gray cloth from their faces, their tongues are wound up around a little stick. They show me the drawings I made as a child: all my clouds are fitted with gills.

Falling Star

Night, and on a desolate road out by the coast a bride and groom come along. There is forest all around them. For a moment they stop, both tilt their heads to one side, at exactly the same angle, to be able to follow the luminous traces that shoot over the winter sky. "Yes, frozen pieces of carbon, cold flames, the salts of the laboratory," they say with one voice. It is just what you could hope for: the wind roars and grinds in the treetops. It sounds like the surf down on the beach. They are all alone in the dark, and the bride's ten-yard veil is flapping between her legs like a long, white beard.

Hair

In the old, now shuttered, barber's shop two previous customers are sitting in the leather-covered barber's chairs. Their faces are caved-in; their clothes much too large for their withered bodies. The most strange, tiny, black insects are crawling out from their rolled up shirt sleeves. The skin on their forearms looks like the finest, white faience, their veins arabesques painted on with ink. The eyes are open. Dust covers their eyelashes. The barber stands washing the hair of one with very slow movements, but the hair falls out in clumps. He sighs, hums a line from a ballade: "Up from blackened mould the hair is growing," and then takes out the scissors.

Angel

An angel on a telephone wire: its vague outline looks like that characteristic, frozen haze, well-known from x-rays of the human body. It swings back and forth like a coy schoolgirl while it picks the lice from its wings. Nevertheless it is said that the water in an angel's body always is close to boiling; that an angel evaporates if it gets so much as a single insect in its eye; but an angel knows nothing of the world, the cruelty or the beauty: inside its skull, on a fishing line, hangs a fizzled star.

Late

It is late, and we go to bed. We lie absolutely still under the thick duvets in the newly washed, slightly stiff, white bed linen, and stare up into space. The chamber pot stands under the bed, the hot-water bottle lies at the baseboard. Our pajamas are utterly identical, striped, and of course a little too big. Only a few would ever recognize that our eyebrows are fake.

Darkness

The apes leap out over the rail, their long arms whirling loose-jointed around their small hairy bodies during the fall through the darkness along the ship's side. Nobody hears them hit the surface. Nobody knows whether the surface exists, or the sea, maybe long since, has disappeared under the ship that is now drifting through clouds of black steam high above oceanic canyons. Nobody wants to know: "After all, we are not apes."

From *Circles* (1998)

Winter

We are naming the birds, and to what use: under the ice of the inlet a skeleton swims with eyes wide-open; at the cemetery the much-too-soon dead lie eating themselves. It is winter, and a bare tree scrapes with its branches on the fire door of the gray sky.

The Photographer

He shouts and gesticulates: wants the tree to come closer. He sees the grass turn a deaf ear, and the puddles pretend they do not reflect anything. Now he has arranged it all: reality has been cut out, the halves joined into a circle, and before long he is on his knees, begging. But it refuses. It stays where it is.

Burne-Jones

On this golden staircase: a procession of women. They carry their musical instruments from clouds made of ether, to be laid among gold and silk, columns of brass. Afterwards they'll remove the clothes from one another's white bodies: soon they're cocoons, each body a labyrinthine wasps' nest, with patterns of wallpaper from deserted houses on the insides of their skin. They descend the staircase. Nobody watches them.

Sleep

While you sleep, the conscious world is cut out of the universe with crooked scissors. Then you see like an animal again, remember with the body: the shadows that rock the children in their long, thin arms; a stretch of highway that's deserted. If the sleep is deep enough, the soul sneaks into the bedroom and lies down a few hours beside your body. Like a betrayed woman who cautiously puts her arms around her sleeping lover.

Flash

This fast: your face lights itself up from the inside, and your eyes smile at me, but your mouth like always is serious, the delicate curves of your lips outlined with a certain disquieting, inscrutable naiveté. The dim cone of the jaw slightly off, as if your head is a statue's with its neck cut through and pushed to the side. The nose blends into the surface of your face, the forehead collapses as if made of the whitest sand. I place a finger on your lips: you do not say a word.

Windows

It isn't enough to lick the windows. It's only when you drill a hole through your hand, and hold it before one of your eyes, that the windows adhere like stamps to the world, returning it to sender. Three million leaves, sixteen trees, a clubhouse, four hundred tombstones, three tennis balls and the Aarhus cathedral will instantly be sucked into the eye. After that, it doesn't matter if someone puts the moon on your tongue like a giant gray pill: you have it all in your head.

Riddle

Like the sea it eats of the cat's paws and repeats the same movement unceasingly. Its body is a white night, its face is a woman's, and the mouth gasps for breath like a fish hauled up into the sun, gleaming and wet. Slowly it closes the sky, with all its heft.

Elephant

When an elephant is left by its darling, it digs itself into the ground until only the outermost part of the trunk is visible. In one region of Tanzania, where the elephant cows are unusually lovely, one finds many elephants with broken hearts. Here trunks seem to shoot up everywhere from the savanna.

Lakmé

In Delibes' opera *Lakmé* the princess Lakmé and her slave-girl Mallika stroll in a large, magic garden. They sing a love song, and we know it is to each other, because we have read about the fondness of the fin de siècle for lesbianism. But it surprises us, even so, when at the end of the scene they disappear into a shining fog of Huygens' cosmic ether: the all-engulfing substance in which light-waves run.

Transformation

If you want to be my Egyptian princess and replace your head with a cat's, I will first, like certain types of octopus, detach an arm to perform the mating ceremony. Afterwards, I'll transform myself into the hieroglyph that means shadow: a dome that hovers over your head atop its long, thin neck firmly posted in the ground.

Spring

The sun lounges in dreamless sleep, the eyes shut, the back in shreds of darkness. It is that night before spring, and in a few hours, when a ribbon of smoke rises from a crack in the ground, the rain will come and the tree roots will begin to loosen their grip on the frost. It is a bit like in the old days: the earth will be set in motion by a winch that stands on a ship whose hull is welded together by stars. For the same reason, there are handles on the clouds so they can be carried out to sea and, once there, become themselves again.

The Poet

He acquires an artificial hand in the shape of a pair of compasses pulled over a glove, and then he draws circles on the paper, until they begin to resemble something he already knew. As if he were a toad that sits staring out at the world. Or to put it another way: or to put it another way.

Dream

When you hang your clothes out to dry, suddenly you know the exact number of languages spoken by the clouds. You can walk around naked in the park, lie down in the grass, and let birds pick your navel deeper: the spleen is the last thing they eat. Soon you are your own ghost, swaying from side to side in the undercurrent of the wind between the houses on the street where you once lived. Before you wake up, the haunt you'll choose will be the world.

Out

The cells of the body are hungry: they bare their sharply pointed teeth and snap at everything that moves. They want to burn up. They want to curl up like electric hedgehogs. They want to be shot from the ears like grand, genetic fireworks and illuminate the emptied sack of the skin as it collapses around the skeleton. Not a shadow of a foot will remain.

Code

The boxes are opened and we dress in red, while people mill through the dark, swinging lanterns. I repeat: we lie awake all night fully dressed in the beds of strangers. Then we're to be bathed, sitting up in large zinc tubs in unfurnished rooms, until a procession carrying burnt out lanterns passes through the street.

Giraffe

When a giraffe falls asleep, it lies stretched out on the ground, almost impossible to awaken. You may choose to step over the giraffe, but if its placement makes waking it necessary, it's possible only by pressing a certain spot on the neck. Regrettably this spot varies from giraffe to giraffe.

Disappearance

With its twenty open decks, the white barge lulls from side to side as passengers take their seats on the benches. When this floating panopticon doesn't capsize, doesn't drag them all down into the black canal, it is due to the lightness of their clothes, their calm movements, and the utter silence all observe. The boat has no sails, and no engine noise is heard, as it leaves the quay and heads out of the harbor.

Liberty

To choose to wake up in one's own body. To get up and go out into town, letting the hand trace the cracks and furrows of the walls, and at every locked door to press the handle down three times before moving on.

The Painter

With a fat brush he paints a white stripe down his otherwise finished painting, dividing up the world with a new, vertical horizon. When he tilts his head to one side, he thinks he might be getting closer.

The Brain

This fungus stretches its mycelium strings all the way up into the clouds, it sucks out their meaning and leaves them ashen and brittle. Like any other sponge it is blind and deaf and will hardly ever be able to see how the light sidles round the corner or hear the chattering birds answer the Morse of the drainpipe: that the rain has stopped. This is why the brain always shrinks in the open air. A few moments of sun will do.

Tanguy

Above the gray sea: a mist of soil where large, drop-shaped bones lie petrified among the flies' wings. And in this dead beehive turned inside-out stand frozen pennants, nodes in time and space, the shadows of other insects. If you walk in this landscape, you will sooner or later encounter the skeletal vestige of the moth's soft back, from which, all the while, the plant you've sought has been growing: a pin.

Awakening

Shadows flow like clouds reflected in lakes under the thin skin of her back. Like medusas hanging under the gleaming roof of the sea, or giant, blind butterflies caught in dusty curtains. Her body is light and thin and white, her hair black and metallic in the cool morning blue that streams through the blinds. In the curve of her back you can make out an animal, drinking. Her porous eyelids shiver. She is on the point of waking.

X-Ray

She uses the tail of a fish skeleton as a fan. Musical tones pour out of her ears and float through the air like droplets; it is a room with no gravity. She dances slowly in place with her three most important tubes: the spine and the windpipe, and the arms, which work as a balancing rod. Together they form three white lines in the dark. Her face is not seen.

Standing

He had always walked upright like a human being and thus wanted to die standing. Not pitifully rattling with shit far up his back and a fat and understanding nurse as the only witness. That is why he had himself tied to the wall and stood there trying to preserve a firm and sharp glance, with his teasingly deriding smile and calm breathing. When finally the floor transformed into sand, the building lay down on its side, and he had to scream his way through all of the hours, it took both the caretaker and his assistant to cram the darkness down his throat.

Question

He can't understand it. His beautiful young wife can't understand it. None of their beautifully designed coffee pots understand it. So we try once more for them: we extend our arms to twice their length, bend them backwards, and walk on their lawn with slow, stylized movements, while we hoot like the very rare, one-eyed Indonesian owl. And still, they're not satisfied: they want the stalk that's left when mathematics has been plucked.

Rhinoceros

When a rhinoceros is born, the animal immediately realizes that it is a big, beautiful and horned head that drags a disproportionately small, gray, and utterly drab body after itself. This is why rhinoceroses spend the rest of their lives running away from their bodies. While doing so, they bump into the world.

Autumn

In October you have more blood in your eyes, see more clearly and do not need to dream about the water, the cold sea and the evenings, where the moon washes ashore like a mine made of brass. The overcoat is already whispering of better days to come: the insoluble equations of the storms and the leathery trees in the parks. The tongues of strangers and the new color of the sand. All the angels will stay tucked in their coffins, their mouths stuffed with leaves.

Man Ray

The lines of her face run like luminous traces under the still surface of a night-dark sea. Her eyes are made of coal, the nose of hydrogen, her skin is early fog. Between the broken oval of her neck and the wavy boundary of her hair lies the white plane of her nape: a piece of marble, meticulously polished. The entire body is focused on a point of balance which is not its own, so she keeps herself floating in the room by resting her head inside her left armpit.

Doze

When we doze in each other's arms, love drifts in its little boat. The only sounds are her breathing against the quiet pulse of the neck, and some rain that falls into an empty glass on the table outside. The rain grinds into the inner face of the glass while the sun sets beneath her eyelids. To stand up is never easy: you hang in rubber bands from the ceiling, slowly dangling, with her hair wrapped round your thighs.

The Ear

The house resounds unbearably; even the coughing of the snails, he hears. And always there are sounds that can't be pinpointed: a gigantic moth trapped in the bedroom, a subterranean river changing its course. Far too much noise in the background to pick up any signal pattern. This is why he cuts off his ear and places it out on the lawn in front of the house.

Florescent Lamp

When everybody lies in their bedrooms like forgotten jackets in the darkness of wardrobes, you sit absolutely still. All night long. Your brain is your eyes, which register the light from the only source in the room. Unconsciously, over and over, you reel off the names of all the inert gases: helium, argon, xenon, radon and neon, thus unable to breathe. When you wake up, it is in a bathtub in a large old bathing room. Because your body has turned into porcelain, you hear the noise from the street in long reverberations, and the light hesitates longer than usual. Then at last you breathe liquid: an entire sea, evaporated.

Incident

It happens at the café, while all the others present sit rocking their tables. It is an autumn day with this beautiful, clear sky that you love, and you've just come in through the door, sat down at a table, and there a woman steps in. She rings a tiny silver bell: it is time.

Hippopotamus

When a hippopotamus dies it lets out a roar, so that the fish fall deaf to the bottom. The hippopotamus is a big inflated stomach covered with a hide, a wonder of nature that floats, eats, fucks and only sweats blood when it's drowsy. The final roar releases all the air. That's why no one has seen a dead hippopotamus.

Then

I met you again at a chemist's up north, tongue-kissed you in the hard, cold light of a basement room. Now you sit on the bed with your hands tied behind you, and a short string from the headboard to your collar. You are singing with two voices, simultaneously and parallel, but with the distance of a fifth. Strange that I did not notice it then, but you have keyholes instead of nipples.

Joining

I took you home with me, here by the harbor, where the fish are poisoned now. Even the widows belch between sentences because of it. Like snow falls through the darkness under streetlights, we fell through each other, and when we woke up this morning, our spines had grown together, so we had to crawl out of bed as a single, huge insect.

Genesis

When the day comes, when I get the idea to turn and look back at myself standing by the lamppost with my three guardian angels, all of them drunk by the light and flying around the lamp in eager discourse over my fate, I am certain that I'll never again write a letter, be advised by a friend, or engage in any talk at dinner. Instead, I'll become human again, I'll discover the small flask with curved forms that is suddenly standing on the bedside table in the morning. I'll insist it wasn't I who put it there.

Acknowledgements

Circumference: "Riddle," "The Ear"

Eleventh Muse: "Fox," "Squirrel"

Exquisite Corpse: "Hippopotamus"

Mid-American Review: "Winter," "Genesis," "Sleep," "Question," "Transformation," "Dream," "Spring," "Awakening," "X-Ray," "Out," "Disappearance," "Joining," "Burne-Jones," "Summer," "Windows," "Elephant," "The Photographer," "Standing," "The Poet," "Autumn"

Mississippi Review: "Teeth," "Hair"

Parthenon West: "Wild Boar," "Rat," "Owl," "Lion"

The Two Lines Anthology: "Spider," "Octopus," "Lizard," "Elephant" and portions of the introductory essay.

Our gratitude to editor and friend, the late Herb Scott, for his support, careful eye, and belief in these poems, and to George Looney at *Mid-American Review* for his early encouragement.

The World Cut Out with Crooked Scissors consists of translations of prose poems from Carsten René Nielsen's three latest books of poetry: *Circles* (*Cirkler,* 1998), *Clairobscur* (2001), and *Forty-One Animals* (*Enogfyrre dyr*, 2005) originally published in Danish by Borgens Forlag, Denmark. www.borgen.dk

Carsten René Nielsen is the author of eight books of poetry, most recently *Forty-One Animals* (2005), which won him critical acclaim throughout his native Denmark. Recent collections include *Circles* (1998) and *Clairobscur* (2001). His first book, *Mechanic Loves Machinist*, was published in 1989, and was awarded the Michael Strunge Prize for Literature. He has won several fellowships from the Danish Council on the Arts. His poetry has been featured in magazines in Italy, Germany, Canada and the United States. Nielsen lives in Aarhus.

David Keplinger's third poetry book, *The Prayers of Others*, was published in 2006. He has been awarded the T.S. Eliot Prize, as well as fellowships from the National Endowment for the Arts, the Pennsylvania Council on the Arts, and the Katey Lehman Foundation. His poems appear in *Ploughshares*, *AGNI*, *Poetry*, *The Iowa Review*, *The Gettysburg Review* and many other journals. Keplinger teaches at American University in Washington, D.C.

New Issues Poetry

David Marlatt, *A Hog Slaughtering Woman*
Louise Mathias, *Lark Apprentice*
Gretchen Mattox, *Buddha Box, Goodnight Architecture*
Paula McLain, *Less of Her; Stumble, Gorgeous*
Lydia Melvin, *South of Here*
Sarah Messer, *Bandit Letters*
Malena Mörling, *Ocean Avenue*
Julie Moulds, *The Woman with a Cubed Head*
Carsten René Nielsen, *The World Cut Out With Crooked Scissors*
Marsha de la O, *Black Hope*
C. Mikal Oness, *Water Becomes Bone*
Bradley Paul, *The Obvious*
Jennifer Perrine, *The Body Is No Machine*
Katie Peterson, *This One Tree*
Elizabeth Powell, *The Republic of Self*
Margaret Rabb, *Granite Dives*
Rebecca Reynolds, *Daughter of the Hangnail, The Bovine Two-Step*
Martha Rhodes, *Perfect Disappearance*
Beth Roberts, *Brief Moral History in Blue*
John Rybicki, *Traveling at High Speeds* (expanded second edition)
Mary Ann Samyn, *Inside the Yellow Dress, Purr*
Ever Saskya, *The Porch is a Journey Different From the House*
Mark Scott, *Tactile Values*
Hugh Seidman, *Somebody Stand Up and Sing*
Heather Sellers, *The Boys I Borrow*
Martha Serpas, *Côte Blanche*
Diane Seuss-Brakeman, *It Blows You Hollow*
Elaine Sexton, *Sleuth*
Marc Sheehan, *Greatest Hits*
Heidi Lynn Staples, *Guess Can Gallop*
Phillip Sterling, *Mutual Shores*
Angela Sorby, *Distance Learning*
Matthew Thorburn, *Subject to Change*
Russell Thorburn, *Approximate Desire*
Rodney Torreson, *A Breathable Light*
Lee Upton, *Undid in the Land of Undone*
Robert VanderMolen, *Breath*
Martin Walls, *Small Human Detail in Care of National Trust*
Patricia Jabbeh Wesley, *Before the Palm Could Bloom: Poems of
    Africa*